中国北京工艺美术展览

To Kwok Hsin Leung and Sam L. Manatt, Jr., in recognition
of the contribution they have made to the development and
strengthening of cultural ties between the United States
of America and the People's Republic of China.

EXHIBITION OF SPECIAL CHINA-PEKING ARTS & CRAFTS

Published by
TAMAR PRODUCTIONS, INC.
Washington D.C., USA

Printed by The Art Litho Company, Baltimore, Maryland, USA

Table of Contents

Table of Contents (Continued)

INTRODUCTION

The artist who labors in Peking today is profoundly conscious of the ancient ideals of classical Chinese art. For the first time in many decades, traditional art is enjoying the active support of the Chinese government. Peking, the center of the arts in contemporary China, is the scene of a vigorous revival of interest in ancient art; its artists and craftsmen are guided and inspired by the time-honored techniques and principles of design that have contributed so much to China's cultural heritage.

Like his ancient counterpart, the modern Chinese artist is heavily influenced by nature. His intimate appreciation of nature and his perception of its spiritual connotations is unparalleled in any other culture. Coupled with this is a painstaking concern with perfection of form and technique.

The individual vision and personal style of the artist is not considered to be of primary importance. Rather, it is his ability to learn from his predecessors and to draw on the vast experience built up by other artists over the centuries. From this stems the fascinating practice of "transforming" or copying the work of earlier artists. Throughout China's history, works of art from one era have been copied in the next, often many times. Modern China is no exception to this custom, and some of the pieces in this collection are precise copies of the work of earlier artists.

This notion, so foreign to those who believe that old art is automatically better than new, and that an original is always better than a replica, has often been seen by westerners as less than acceptable artistic practice.

In China, however, the art of "transforming" is an entirely honorable and conscious practice and does not suggest any lack of initiative or originality on the part of the artist. It is based on the assumption that the copier will in some way inherit the genius of the artist who made the original. At the same time, the artist will sometimes strive to improve on the work he is copying. This leads in turn to the conclusion that a perfect modern replica of a fine antique art work is, in its own right, a unique artistic entity and can somehow represent a distillation of the total experience in that art form that has been accumulated through the ages.

This traditional approach to arts and crafts has only recently been revived in China. In the 19th Century, the art forms that had flourished for so many eras began to decline in quality. The demand for exports to the western world meant that items were often hurriedly produced. At the same time, the demand for craftsmen to produce western-style goods did little to advance traditional Chinese art.

In the troubled early years of the 20th Century, art and craft-work was largely neglected. It was not until the early 50's that the new Government of the People's Republic of China began to set up training centers where old, experienced craftsmen could pass on their skills to the young. At this time, emphasis was placed on reviving traditional techniques, while the designs focused on modern revolutionary themes.

During the Cultural Revolution of the late 60's, many antique works of art were branded as bourgeois and decadent, and duly destroyed. After the purges of that era, the old traditional designs were reinstated and were accorded due significance for their place in China's art heritage. In recent years, the establishment of new museums and the emphasis given by the Government to archaeological research has greatly encouraged interest in traditional designs for arts and crafts.

The common theme in the collection illustrated here is this revival of traditional designs. Some of these represent philosophical ideas; some are scenes derived from literature. Others make use of ancient religious symbolism. In order to appreciate the artists' intentions, some basic understanding is needed of the significance of these symbols.

Usually representing natural or supernatural forces, symbols were originally thought to protect against evil spirits and to confer certain blessings. The most sought-after blessings were immortality, longevity, and material prosperity.

The best known symbols relate to ancient Chinese philosophy. This was based on belief in the "T'ai Ji", the source of existence, which produced the two principles that in turn created all things in nature. The principles are the "yang", the active male principle, and the "yin", the passive female principle. The "T'ai Ji" is often represented by a simple circle divided in half by a curved line.

From the "yang" springs all the active elements and the active forces in nature, all of which are represented by symbols. Among the most ancient of these is the thunder and cloud pattern symbolizing the gods who brought rain to the crops. To a people so dependent on agriculture, the life-giving rain was seen as one of the most important blessings bestowed by the gods. Originally a primitive spiral pattern, the thunder and clouds appear in more recent art forms as an angular design often used in borders. It is seen on the corners of the carriage in the *Phoenix Lantern Carriage* (page 69).

Perhaps the best known symbols are those of the four sacred, supernatural creatures: the dragon, the phoenix, the unicorn, and the tortoise. The dragon, seen on pages 31, 37, 45, 51, and 66, stands for the renewal of life in spring and for productivity. This fabled creature also controls rainfall and floods and rules over the east. The phoenix, pages 39, 45, 48, 65, and 69, appears only when the land is at peace. This king of birds represents the joys and warmth of summer and rules over the south. The dragon and the phoenix are also the respective emblems of the Emperor and the Empress. The unicorn influences maturity in autumn and controls the west. The tortoise rules the north, controls the winter, and symbolizes longevity, strength, and endurance. When these creatures appear in Chinese art work, their precise meaning is determined by their context. For example, the *Six-Armed Buddha Locking Up the Flood Dragon* (page 37), is intended to show

man's determination to conquer and control nature. The Buddha is shown holding a lock and various treasures and seals suggesting power and strength; the dragon, representing floods, is shown in a submissive position, bound by the Buddha's chain.

The hare, seen in the carving on page 42, like the fox, stands for long life; the red hare appears as an auspicious omen when a virtuous ruler is governing the country. The magpie (page 60) is the bird of joy, whose presence is considered a sign of good luck. The goat (page 68), like the ram and sheep, is a symbol of filial piety.

Besides the animals, many mythical characters appear in Chinese art. Among the most popular are the "Eight Immortals", Taoist representations of people who have attained immortality. Each Immortal has his own emblem; for example, a

flute, a fan, a pair of castanets. These favored beings are often pictured sailing across the sea toward paradise or already in paradise enjoying the delights of immortality. In the agate carving on page 51, three of the Immortals are shown battling with, and setting fire to the dragon of the eastern sea, who is attempting to hinder their progress toward paradise.

Another popular legendary figure who appears frequently in Chinese art is Xi Wang Mu, the fairy Queen of the Sky. Xi Wang Mu is a Taoist figure who lives in splendor, attended by fairies, at a palace near the Lake of Gems. On the shore of this lake grows a fabulous immortal peach tree. According to legend, the tree bears fruit only once in 3,000 years. Those who are fortunate enough to eat of these peaches gain the desired immortality. In the agate/jade carving on page 50, the fairies are celebrating longevity and immortality on the

occasion of Xi Wang Mu's birthday. They are seen gathered around a precious gourd which rests on the crest of an ocean wave.

Of all the flowers and trees favored by Chinese artists, the peach is probably the best known. As well as conferring immortality, it represents longevity and marriage. The peony, another favorite, is seen as the king of flowers and an omen of good fortune. However, if the peony flower unexpectedly withers, disaster or poverty will befall its owner. The plum and the pine are often pictured together, as in the coral carving on page 49. The two are seen as symbols of friendship and constancy, because the pine remains green in winter while the plum tree blossoms from leafless branches. The chrysanthemum (page 43) symbolizes mid-autumn and is an emblem of pleasure and good cheer.

Many Chinese artists draw on the classics of Chinese literature for their inspiration. A number of the pieces shown here depict scenes from *A Dream of Red Mansions*, an 18th Century epic novel written by Cao Xueqin. Regarded by western critics as one of the great classics of all literature, it paints a vast panorama of life in China during the decline of the Qing Dynasty. The novel exposes the inherent corruption and immorality of Chinese feudal society, seen through the lives of members of the powerful, aristocratic Jia family.

The complex plot centers on a tragic love affair between Lin Daiyu (Black Jade) and her cousin Jia Baoyu. Lin Daiyu is a fragile, chaste, and beautiful orphan who refuses to be contaminated by the evil she finds around her; but confronted with a society where polygamy and arranged marriages

are the norm, she is powerless to control her own fate. As the story unfolds, she becomes increasingly absorbed in unbearable sorrow and self-pity. Baoyu, the family's second son, is a champion of oppressed women. In expressing his love for Daiyu, he rebels against the prevailing social and moral order. In the novel's tragic conclusion, Baoyu is forced into marrying another cousin, Baochai (Precious Clasp). Weakened by consumption and overwhelmed with grief, Lin Daiyu dies on the night of their wedding. Baoyu, in a final act of rebellion, renounces the world and becomes a monk.

There are hundreds of characters and a vast array of richly drawn scenes in *A Dream of Red Mansions*. Many of these are household favorites in China today. In *Daiyu Buries the Flowers* (page 55), Lin Daiyu, already stricken with consumption, is seen sorrowfully burying the dying petals of the plum blossoms. Lamenting her own short life expectancy, she wonders who will care for her remains when she is gone.

In a happier scene (page 54), Lin Daiyu is watching Baoyu and his cousin and future bride, Baochai, playing chess. Baoyu is undecided on his next move. After studying the board carefully, Lin Daiyu suggests a move he should make, which enables him to win the game.

In the carving on page 57, another of Baoyu's cousins, Baoqin, is seen in the snow with her maid, Yahuan, who is carrying a vase of red plum blossoms. The scene takes place one snowy day in early spring when the cousins have had a session of drinking wine and writing light-hearted poems. Slightly tipsy, Baoqin sets out wearing a precious cape made of wild duck down, that was given to her by the Jia family matriarch. She decides to fetch plum blossoms to inspire their poetry writing. The enchanting picture of the beautiful girl with the red blossoms against white snow has been a favorite subject among Chinese artists.

Xi Xiang-yun, the silk figure on page 72, is another of Baoyu's cousins and a popular and lively character in the story. The scene, represented in silk on page 73, comes from an episode where Baochai, after running through the garden in pursuit of a butterfly, overhears Baoyu's maidservant attempting to blackmail another young girl.

A scene from another popular Chinese classic is depicted in the jade carving on page 40. *The Western Chamber* takes its story from a romantic tale called "The Story of Ying Ying", originally written by 7th Century poet Yuan Zhen. It tells of the love affair of Cui Ying Ying, a bewitchingly beautiful girl, and a talented young scholar, Chang Sheng.

Yuan Zhen's story ended in tragedy with Chang Sheng's desertion of Ying Ying. In the 12th Century, Imperial poet Dong Jie-yuan developed the story into a lengthy lyrical drama and gave it a happy ending. Ying Ying and Chang appear as idealized lovers in numerous plays and novels based on Dong's version of the story. The most celebrated of these is a 20 act play by another 13th Century writer, Wang Shi-fu. Always a popular play, Wang's romantic and humorous *Western Chamber* enjoyed a period of notoriety in the 18th Century, when it was considered improper reading for young people.

In the scene on page 40, Ying Ying is accompanied by her maid, an inveterate matchmaker named Hong Niang. The two have come to the garden to burn incense to the spirit of Ying Ying's departed father. Deep in prayer, Ying Ying is unaware of the presence of the lovesick Chang, who is watching her from behind the garden wall. Inscribed on the carving is a poem which expresses Chang's love for Ying Ying.

For the Chinese artist, the materials he chooses to use have as much historical significance as the subjects he seeks to portray. Since earliest times, jade, "the stone of heaven", has been accorded a special place in Chinese art mythology and has been regarded by the Chinese as the most precious of all materials, more valuable even than gold.

As a craft, jade carving is among the most ancient known to man. Prehistoric peoples carved jade into weapons, utensils, and tools; in historical times the Chinese, the Mayas, the Aztecs, and the Maoris made ornaments and jewelry of jade. It was in China, however, that the art of jade carving became the most highly developed. By the 12th Century B.C., during the Zhou Dynasty, it had become an established and sophisticated craft in China. Carved jade served as currency; it was used for ornaments denoting princely rank and for sacrificial offerings to the gods. Jade ground into powder was eaten by kings and princes as an act of religious purification. In the excavations of the Man Cheng tombs, the bodies of a Han Dynasty (205 B.C. - 220 A.D.) prince and his consort were found clad from head to toe in suits made of finely carved jade pieces, held together with gold and silver thread.

The ancients used jade in this manner because they believed it possessed divine powers. It was thought to be able to cure illness, to ward off evil and misfortune, to prevent decay after death, and even to triumph over death. At the same time, the ancients ascribed five virtues to jade: charity, wisdom, rectitude, courage, and equity.

All these attributes stemmed from the stone's exceptional beauty, its rarity, and its remarkable physical properties. The term jade covers two distinct mineral groups. nephrite and jadeite. Jadeite, which was not used in China until the 18th Century, is the harder of the two; but its chemical structure makes it slightly easier to cut than nephrite. Both of these extremely tough crystalline stones rank in hardness close to a diamond and both offer a formidable resistance to the carver's tools.

Both nephrite and jadeite range in color from white to black, the thousands of shades of coloring being formed by the presence of iron compounds and other chemicals in the stone. A high iron content, for example, makes for the darkest greens and blacks; when free of extraneous chemicals, both nephrite and jadeite are pure white. Of the nephrites, the white "mutton fat" color, seen on page 31, and the "spinach" green flecked with a darker color are the most highly prized by the Chinese. Of the colors found in jadeite, the "moss entangled in the melting snow" or white mottled with emerald green is considered the most precious color. The soft, sea-green color seen in the *Elephant Pedestal Vase* (page 35) and the bright, almost translucent green in *The Western Chamber* (page 40) are also highly sought after.

Once the stone is carved and polished, it is virtually impossible to tell the difference between jadeite and nephrite, and the same criteria are used to assess the general quality of the stones. Apart from color, these criteria include the jade's smoothness, its coolness to the touch, and its sound. Chimes carved of jade were once used in Imperial and religious ceremonies; struck with an ebony mallet, the chimes would produce deep sonorous tones.

The rarity of jade, which has seldom been found within China's borders, has added greatly to its value. China's main sources of jade over the centuries have been in the rivers and mountains of Turkestan, Siberia, and Burma. Huge blocks of jade have been found in mountain mines, while jade pebbles and boulders are found in rivers and streams. According to one early account, women were sometimes made to strip and wade in the rivers in search of jade. It was believed that jade embodied the "yang" or male principle and would, therefore, be attracted to women, who embodied the opposite "yin" principle. Today jade is extracted from mines in a somewhat more sophisticated manner.

Early records give little information about the methods and tools used by the ancient jade carvers. Apart from a desire to preserve the secrets of the craft, it is thought that the scholarly writers of those days preferred not to mention manual labor. Among the few available writings on the subject are accounts of magical knives and a mystery substance known as "toad-grease" that was thought to reduce the jade to a workable medium. Less fanciful accounts describe various rotating tools, garnet tipped drills, and knives made of galvanized iron, which were used in conjunction with abrasives mixed with grease.

Modern Chinese artists employ much the same techniques and tools to work this unyielding material, though many of the modern drills are diamond-pointed and driven by electricity. After the outer "skin" of the stone is removed with a saw, the excess material is ground away; and a design is drawn onto the jade. Carvers then sculpt the remaining stone with a variety of hand tools. The majority of the close carving work is done with a blade and abrasives. Particular skills such as drilling out a hollow vase or carving moveable ring handles or chain links, as seen in the *Great Eastern Dragon Floral Censer* (page 31), are performed by specialists who may devote their entire careers to that one operation.

The final process is a rigorous polishing. A mysterious substance called "pao yao" is smeared onto leather buffing tools, which are designed to reach into seemingly inaccessible areas. The end result is a durable, waxlike shine. Hand in hand with the old techniques go certain ancient principles that govern the art of jade carving. These principles, well illustrated in the carvings on pages 29, 33, and 43, are: to select the theme according to the materials, to allow the shape and varied coloring of the stone to dictate the design, and to reveal the stone's qualities while hiding its defects.

Hardstone carving techniques cover work with many different substances. These range from jade, agate, turquoise, malachite, and rose quartz, to coral, rock crystal, and lapis lazuli. While these stones all vary in texture and hardness, they respond to tools in the same general manner as jade. Of the group, coral and turquoise merit special attention, because of the difficulties they create for the craftsmen.

Coral has been widely used in jewelry, ornaments for the hair, and for headdresses, as in the crown on the head of the phoenix in *Phoenix Lantern Carriage* (page 69). The brittleness of coral, however, makes it extremely difficult to carve finely. For this reason, the carving on page 37 is an outstanding example of the art.

Turquoise presents even more complex problems for the craftsman. Its composition is such that it cannot be subjected to any kind of heat or friction, nor can it be immersed in water. Even exposure to light or open air for any length of time can affect the stone's color and its finish. These properties severely limit the type of tools that can be used by the craftsmen. *Floral Vase* (page 47) demonstrates how Chinese carvers have been able to overcome these difficulties.

The art of carving ivory dates back to the Shang Dynasty of the 16th Century B.C., when the importance of the material ranked closely with that of gold and jade. By the 11th Century B.C., when most ancient peoples were still eating with their fingers, aristocrats in China were dining with delicately carved ivory chopsticks. Although ivory did not have the magical qualities associated with jade, it was seen as a symbol of status and wealth. A scholar, writing in the First Century A.D., describes some of the many ways in which ivory was used to denote status: "The courtesans dip their slender fingers in ivory boxes containing perfumed cosmetics; the gourmets carry with them their own little ivory sticks for eating rice and the new rich hang their hats on ivory hatstands. Men of the world admire their favorite crickets through the delicate fretwork of ivory forming the lids of special boxes carved out of gourds."

China's ancient center of the ivory carving industry was Nantao, a district of Shanghai. An ivory shop there would employ an entire family, who would produce everyday items such as combs and chopsticks. The family's more proficient carvers would fill orders for special customers. Usually the subject matter of these works would be detailed mythical scenes or figures which required more intricate skills.

Ivory was obtained primarily from the elephant, but also from the mammoth, the walrus, and the narwhal. China used to have large herds of elephants but over the centuries these were slowly driven south by hunters, and merchants had to make journeys to Burma, India, and even Africa, where the most valuable elephant ivory is still found.

The skills involved in carving ivory are similar to those required for hardstone carving. Abrasives are not needed, however, since ivory is relatively soft. Peking artists, who devised the complex technique of coloring ivory with dyes and pigments, as seen in "Bitter-Melon Cricket Box" (page 61), have long been recognized for their high level of achievement in ivory carving. One of the difficulties faced by the craftsman is that each ivory carving can only be fashioned from a single tusk, and the design must be made to fit its contours. This is the basis of a legendary story about a ruler who commanded that a life-size statue be made of him in ivory. This tale of ignorance is the Chinese equivalent of the story of Marie Antoinette and the cake.

One of the key elements in fine ivory carving in ancient China was the use of the grain in the design. This has been revived recently as a result of the high standards now being demanded of artists by the Government of the People's Republic of China.

The techniques involved in working with enamels on metal were first introduced into China by the Arabs in the time of Marco Polo and Kublai Khan. Cloisonne, a method of decorating a surface by enclosing enamel in small wirework cells, was quickly adopted by Peking artists, who developed the technique into a uniquely Chinese art form. Craftsmen in Peking today still use the same techniques that were perfected by their 14th Century counterparts.

A base material, often copper, is first hammered into the shape of the finished product. Thin copper wire is then fashioned into designs of flowers, animals, or geometric patterns. This intricate work is dusted with silver powder and fired so that the wire forms enclosed spaces or "cloisons". The enamel is produced from a glass-like substance which is powdered, sifted, mixed with water, and finally colored. Chinese writing brushes are used to transfer the

enamel into empty spaces; the piece is then fired, causing the enamel to contract. Two or more fillings and firings are required until the cells are completely filled. After polishing with charcoal, the piece is ready for gilding. This involves putting gold into a solution and producing the correct electrolytic reaction. When the piece is immersed in the solution, gold adheres to the exposed surfaces of the copper wire. The final result, of which *Floral Vase* (page 63) is a classic example, is a mosaic-like effect with an even, flawless finish.

Of the many skills involved in cloisonne work, it is in the production of certain colors that Chinese artists have achieved distinction. Of these, one of the most popular is a clear peacock blue, known as "Jingtai Blue", which is seen at its best in *Phoenix Wine Vessel* (page 65). The color takes its name from the

Ming Dynasty Emperor Jingtai (1450-1456 A.D.), during whose era the use of this color flourished.

Cloisonne work is frequently inlaid with other materials such as gold, silver, and precious or semi-precious stones, as seen in *Dragon-Handle Censer* (page 66), *Scenic Floral Censer* (page 71), and *Phoenix Lantern Carriage* (page 69). They combine a number of traditional crafts including cloisonne, chisel engraving, inlays of malachite and turquoise, filigree work, and jade and coral carvings. In *Goats* (page 68), spun gold filigree is inlaid with gems, while the horns and tails are carved of jade.

The silk figures shown on pages 72 and 73 are examples of a new folk craft which has become very popular in modern China. The craft combines traditional designs with modern materials and techniques. The framework of each figure is made of lead wire padded with cotton. The head is covered with silk, then hand painted and finished with hair made of fine silk yarn. The embroidered silk costumes are painted with minutely detailed designs and decorated with tiny pearls secured with gold thread. Much care is taken to ensure that these costumes and their ornaments accurately reflect the fashions of a particular period.

The silk flowers seen at the base of the figures on pages 72 and 73 represent a much older Chinese craft. It is believed that these were first made in the Tang Dynasty (618 - 907 A.D.), during the reign of the Emperor Xianzong. According to legend, his consort, Yang Yuhai, had a scar on her left temple. Every day she would have her court maidens pick fresh flowers which she would wear at the side of her hair to disguise the scar. In winter, the maidens would make flowers for her out of silk. These silk flowers, which are still made by hand today, are considered by the Chinese to be superior to fresh flowers.

Of the many ancient crafts maintained by Peking artists, carved lacquerware stands out as uniquely Chinese. Lacquerware was first used in China some two thousands years ago for preserving everyday objects such as leather shoes, pottery vessels, and even bamboo baskets. Utensils were made from lacquer-soaked cloth which was molded around a wooden model and allowed to dry. From these humble origins, lacquerwork developed over the centuries into a highly sophisticated craft.

The material itself is a type of varnish which is removed from the Rhus vernicifera, a cousin of the sumac bush. The lac is strained, heated by the sun, and stirred to the correct consistency. The famous cinnabar red is produced by grinding sulfide of mercury with the lac, which pigments the material. In the same manner, malachite produces green lacquer, and yellow is produced from ground hartite. Excavations from as early as 476 B.C. have shown that lacquer has a remarkable capacity to retain its color.

To produce carved lacquer, the craftsman must apply between 30 and 200 coats of lac to a wooden base, until sufficient thickness is achieved to sustain relief work. Each thin coating must be thoroughly dry before the next layer is applied. This preparation can take up to two years to complete. The piece must be carved while the final, thickest layer of lacquer is still soft enough to be cut evenly. The carving techniques used in *Flower Basket Plate* (page 75) demonstrate the Chinese artists' ability to create an impression of depth with only 4 cm (1.57 inches) of lacquer.

The ancient tools, the traditional artistic techniques, and the themes from earlier dynasties are for the Chinese an important link with a rich cultural past. But they also represent one of the world's last remaining examples of truly great hand craftmanship. As the Chinese reach out to the technologies of the industrialized world, their Government is taking care to preserve and promote the nation's traditional artistic skills. Its policy stands as an example to all nations whose cultural heritage is threatened by the growing challenges posed by modern industrial development.

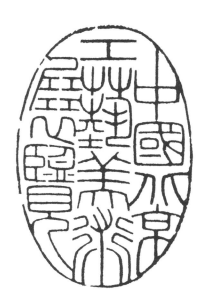

Three Autumn Vase

Rare, varicolored emerald jade. The vase is designed to present a three-sided view of the autumn harvest theme. The cricket, cucumber, lentils, gourd, flowers, latticework and the "bianmeng" (dream changing) plant are carved in deep and shallow relief to harmonize with the stone's natural shape, and to highlight its unique color pattern.
Designed by Wang Zhongyuan.

玉雕翡翠三秋瓶 《珍品》

Great Eastern Dragon Floral Censer

Carved from flawless white jade, the cover is surmounted by a ferocious dragon finial hung with loose rings, and engraved with the images of four famous Chinese scientists amid flower clusters and peony patterns. The peony handles are carved in high relief and hung with moveable rings. The base is engraved with patterns of books, a sword, a spade and a weather instrument, symbols of the scientists. Designed by Xia Changxin.

玉雕白玉东方巨龙花薰《珍品》

Prawn Plate

Carved from a single piece of
semi-translucent agate-opal. The
natural colors and shape dictated
the design. The plate is engraved
with a stylized leaf pattern; the
free-standing prawn is carved in
high relief.

玉雕玛瑙俏色虾盘 《珍品》

Elephant Pedestal Vase

Rare, highly-prized emerald jade. The lid is crested with a finely-engraved elephant, the body carved with a frieze of archaistic dragon and cloud patterns. The elephant-head handles are hung with loose rings.

玉雕翡翠象垒 《珍品》

Six-Armed Buddha Locking Up the Flood Dragon

Carved in high relief from a
single piece of "wawaqiang"
(baby-faced color) coral,
this represents the legendary
theme of man's determination to
conquer and control nature. The
Buddha, adorned with finely-
engraved ribbons and necklace,
holds a lock, treasures and seals,
suggesting power and strength;
the defeated dragon, who symbolizes floods, is bound by the
Buddha's chain. The carving of
the moveable chain from the very
brittle coral represents a
remarkable achievement in this
art form.
Designed by Pan Bingheng.
Produced by Liu Honian

玉雕珊瑚六臂佛锁蛟龙《珍品》

Phoenix Tea Pitcher

White jade. On the body are carved two nymphs derived from a Tang Dynasty painting. One plays a flute, the other a sea shell horn. A phoenix head forms the separate spout cover.

玉雕白玉凤壶 《珍品》

The Western Chamber

Semi-translucent jasper jade, in deep and shallow relief. This depicts a scene from a 13th Century play, "The Western Chamber". The heroine, Ying Ying, and her maid, Hong Niang, are praying and burning incense in the garden. Watching from above and unseen by Ying Ying, is her lovesick admirer, Chang Sheng. Engraved on the carving is a poem expressing Chang's love for the girl.

玉雕碧玉西厢记 《珍品》

Clam Shell Deity

The figure represents Guan Yin, the Buddhist Goddess of Mercy. The bare neck and breast, traditionally very un-Chinese in style, is a tribute to her Indian origin. Of highly polished agate, the figure is carved against a translucent pearl shell background, and stands on a base of engraved stylized waves. In one hand she holds the mythical Luminous Pearl, in the other a "ling- zhi" fungus, purported to cure all illnesses. On her neck is a beaded necklace.

玉雕玛瑙蚌佛 《珍品》

Flowering Crabapple and Little Hare

Varicolored agate, carved in deep relief. The wax-like shine is produced with the aid of a mineral compound called "pao yao", the formula of which is a well kept secret.

玉雕玛瑙俏色海棠小兔《珍品》

Chrysanthemum Vase

Rare Xiuyan jade, highly prized
for its translucency and gold-
green colorings. The chrysanthemum pattern, symbolic of
mid-autumn, is carved against the
body of the vase in deep relief,
the leaves incised with fine veins.

玉雕岫玉俏色菊花瓶　　《珍品》

Dragon Phoenix Jar

Carved from coral, this ceremonial vessel displays the respective emblems of the Emperor and Empress. A phoenix head forms the lidded spout. A fighting dragon entwined around the handle spouts water on the lower dragon, whose body clings to the side of the jar as he is forced down into the sea.

玉雕珊瑚龙凤壶 《珍品》

Floral Vase

Turquoise. With separate dome,
the body is carved in shallow
relief with a strapwork band, and
in deep relief with peonies, plum
blossoms and birds. Because of its
complex composition turquoise
requires extremely delicate handl-
ing. This carving is therefore considered to be an exceptional
technical accomplishment.

玉雕松石花卉瓶 《珍品》

Phoenix Wine Vessel

White jade and jasper jade. The vessel, which rests on a stylized phoenix base, has a separate cover and moveable ring handles. The border on the lip is inlaid with rubies and jade.

玉雕白玉碧玉凤尊 《珍品》

Song of Praise to the Pine and the Plum

Highly polished coral. The design is carved in deep relief against the background of an ox horn cup and tea pitcher. The evergreen pine and blossoming plum are often pictured together as symbols of friendship and constancy.

玉雕珊瑚松梅颂

Hanging Flower Basket

Varicolored emerald jade, utilizing a jade carving technique recently developed in Peking. The original stone was half the height of the final carving; the moveable pendant chains hung with engraved lotus buds and flowers, and the basket filled with leaves and blossoms surmounted by a cricket, are all carved from a single piece of jade.

玉雕翡翠吊樑花籃

50

The Immortals Burning the Sea

玉雕玛瑙俏色八仙烧海

Varicolored crystalline agate. Three of the immortals are shown bearing their respective emblems: at the left He Xian-Gu carries a lotus pod; in the center the chief of the Eight Immortals, Han Zhong- Li holds a fan; at the right is Lu Dong-Bin with his sword. The three are setting fire to the sea to ward off the dragon who is attempting to hinder their progress towards paradise.

Band of Fairies
at Longevity Ceremony

Crystalline agate, jasper jade. The rarely found water marks in this agate were formed naturally over tens of thousands of years. To utilize the stone's features the artists chose the theme of the fairies (immortals), each bearing his or her special emblem, gathered around a precious gourd at a longevity celebration. Misty clouds and gliding cranes surround the gourd which rests on the crest of an ocean wave carved of jasper jade. The wood base is in the shape of a large sea tortoise.

玉雕水胆玛瑙群仙祝寿

Confrontation in Chess

牙雕 红楼 对奕

Ivory, Paint. From a scene in the novel, "A Dream of Red Mansions", Lin Daiyu watches Baoyu and his future bride, Baochai, playing chess. Baoyu is on the verge of losing, but a move suggested by Daiyu enables him to win the game.

Daiyu Buries the Flowers

Carved and painted ivory. Depicting a scene from the classic 18th Century Chinese novel, "A Dream of Red Mansions". The novel's tragic heroine, Lin Daiyu, tearfully buries the fallen plum blossoms as she contemplates her own fate in the corrupt feudal society of that era and wonders who will weep for her when she is gone.

牙雕黛玉葬花

55

Treading the Snow in Search of a Plum Flower

Ivory, paint. The carving is based on another scene from the novel, "A Dream of Red Mansions". Baoqin, one of the novel's principal characters, stands in the snow dressed in a precious duck-down cape. Accompanied by her maid, Yahuan, who carries the vase, Baoqin is searching for plum blossoms as inspiration for a poem she is writing.

牙雕踏雪寻梅《宝琴》

Flower Basket

Ivory, paint. The pierced lattice-work basket features chrysan-themums and plum blossoms carved in high relief. This choice of subject represents a new trend in ivory carving developed by craftsmen in Peking.

牙雕花卉花籃

Magpie Perched
on a Plum Flower

牙雕花卉喜鹊登梅

Ivory, paint. Two magpies, symbols of joy and good fortune, perch on the branches of a flowering plum tree which grows around a fragment of bamboo mingled with pine branches. The plum, pine and bamboo are often pictured together, representing constancy and longevity. When a magpie appears with these three it means that a marriage is about to take place.

牙雕蛐蛐（蟋蟀）赖瓜盒

Bitter-Melon Cricket Box

Ivory, paint, dyes. The theme is derived from the ancient and still popular Chinese sport of cricket fighting. The crickets were kept in cages carved out of bitter-melons or gourds and covered with lids of finely fretted ivory.

Court Lady
Holding Flowers

Ivory, paint. The 18th Century courtesan carries an arrangement of tree peonies, symbolizing spring. Her intricately detailed head dress, ornaments and jewels accurately reflect the fashions of that era.

牙雕持花仕女

Floral Vase

Steel-based cloisonne. Formed with steel wire and bordered with brass, the stylized flower pattern displays the rich array of colors achieved by Chinese enamel artists. The techniques used by the artists to produce unique colors in enamel have earned Chinese cloisonne its distinctive reputation.

景泰兰钢花瓶

Phoenix Wine Vessel

Copper-based, gilded and inlaid with enamel, gold, coral and turquoise. The horn-shaped cup has a phoenix head turned sharply back in Ming style, and crested with a gold crown inlaid with coral. The eyes and two fringed gold bands around the neck and body are inlaid with turquoise. Gold monster masks adorn the wings and tail. The enamel, which features the famous "Jingtai" color (peacock blue) was inlaid in the cloisonne method.

景泰兰鸟尊

Dragon-Handle Censer

Silver, inlaid with enamel, coral, turquoise and agate. Spheres of carved agate are held in the mouths of the two dragon heads on the handle and spout. Friezes in cloisonne of archaistic elephants and a stylized leaf pattern surround the body and cover of the censer, which rests on bird-mask feet.

《银胎》景泰兰龙柄薰

Floral Censer

Silver, enamel, turquoise, semi-precious stones. The body of the censer is decorated with stylized dragon-masks and flower patterns in cloisonne, featuring the famous "jingtai" blue color. The floral handles and ornate crest of the censer are hung with silver rings and inlaid with semi-precious stones.

《银胎》景泰兰花薰

Goats

The horns are made of carved jade, the body of spun gold inlaid with rubies and emeralds.

金嵌宝石羊

Phoenix Lantern Carriage

"Jingtai Blue" and other enamels, gold, silver, malachite, turquoise, coral and jade. The piece combines a number of ancient crafts including cloisonne, hardstone carving, and wire inlaying (on the lantern roof). The phoenix is crested in coral, its feathers and tail inlaid with malachite and turquoise. Jade pendants hang from the carriage, and carved jade is inlaid into the lantern which is surmounted by miniature mythical creatures.

景泰兰凤灯车

Scenic Floral Censer

Silver, enamel, turquoise, malachite, coral, jade and agate. The scenes, formed of silver filigree and enamel, represent the Behai Park and the famous Fuxian Tower of the Summer Palace. Four small phoenixes support the base; two larger phoenixes form the handle. At the top of the censer a peacock inlaid with gems stands on a hill of carved turquois. Very highly prized for its delicate workmanship, the censer combines styles characteristic of the Ming and Qing Dynasties. Designed by Bi Shangpeng and Chai Deshou.

Xi Xiang Yun

This figure represents a character from the classical Chinese novel, "A Dream of Red Mansions". The body is formed in lead wire, padded with cotton, covered and dressed in hand-painted silk. The hair is of fine silk yarn, the tiny pearls and other gemstone ornaments are secured with gold thread. Her costume is an accurate copy of a style worn by 18th Century Chinese courtesans.

绢人史湘云　　《红楼梦人物》

Baochai Chasing a Butterfly

A silk figure depicting a principal character from "A Dream of Red Mansions". In this scene, Baochai runs through the garden in pursuit of an enormous jade- colored butterfly

绢人宝钗扑蝶　　《红楼梦人物》

Flower Basket Plate

Carved in cinnabar lacquer on a base of wood. A year's work and over a hundred coats of lacquer were required to produce the 4cm (1.57 inches) thickness of this piece. The craftsman spent another twelve months on the intricate process of carving and engraving the flower pattern into the lacquer.
Designed by Lin Bingchen.

雕漆花篮盘

Sources

Carter, Michael. *Crafts of China.* Garden City, N.Y., Doubleday, 1977.

Ch'en Shou-yi. *Chinese Literature: A Historical Introduction.* New York, The Ronald Press Co., 1961.

Fodor, Eugene. *Peoples Republic of China.* New York, David McKay Co., Inc., 1979.

Froncek, T., Ed. *Horizon Book of the Arts of China.* New York, American Heritage, 1969.

Garner, Sir Harry M. *Chinese & Japanese Cloisonne-Enamels.* 2nd ed., London, Faber & Faber, Ltd., 1970.

Hansford, S.H. *Chinese Jade Carving.* London, Humphries, 1950.

Ho Chi-fang. "The Dream of the Red Chamber," *Chinese Literature.* Peking, Foreign Languages Press, 1963.

Nott, Stanley Charles. *Chinese Jade Throughout the Ages: A Review of its Characteristics, Decoration, Folklore, and Symbolism.* 2nd ed., Tokyo & Rutland, Vt., C. E. Tuttle Co., 1962.

Strong, Hilda Arthurs. *A Sketch of Chinese Arts & Crafts.* 2nd rev. ed., Peking, Henry Vetch Publishers, 1933.

Tsao Hsueh-chin & Kao Ngo. *A Dream of Red Mansions.* Translated by Hsien-yi Yang and Gladys Yang, Peoples Republic of China, Peking, Foreign Languages Press, 1978.

Wheeldon, Beryl M. "China's Arts & Crafts." Hong Kong, *Eastern Horizon*, vol. 5: #3, 1966.

Notes & Descriptions on the Exhibit: Translated from notes by Peking Arts & Crafts Industrial Corporation, Peking, People's Republic of China, 1979.

Xrandai Hanyu Cidian. *Modern Chinese Dictionary* Peking, Commercial Press of China, 1977.

Photo Credits

Page 9, Soochou. Photo by M. Durrance/Black Star. *Page 10.* Photo courtesy of the Peoples Republic of China. *Page 11,* Canal in Canton. Photo by Nik Wheeler/Black Star. *Page 12,* Marble Boat, Summer Palace, Peking. Photo by Terry Madison/Image Bank. *Page 12,* Tortise, Chinese symbol of Long Life, Peking. Photo by Terry Madison/Image from Peking painting a scene from the Great Wall. Photo by M. Durrance/Black Star. *Page 15,* Tien-An-Men Square, Peking. Photo by Emil Schulthes/Black Star. *Page 16,* LiKiang/Kwangsi. Photo by Emil Schulthes/Black Star. *Page 17,* Artist, government Arts & Crafts factory, Foshan. Photo by Terry Madison/Image Bank. *Page 18,* Ivory Carvers. Photo courtesy of the Peoples Republic of China. *Page 20,* Soochou. Photo by M. Durrance/Black Star. *Page 21,* Silk Embroidery, Soochou. Photo by M. Durrance/Black Star. *Page 21, Close up of ornamented tile roof in Peking. Photo by M. Durrance/Black Star. Page 21,* Commune near Kweilin. Photo by Terry Madison/Image Bank. *Page 22,* Lily Pads, Summer Palace, Peking. Photo by Terry Madison/Image Bank. *Page 23,* Making Silk Figures. Photo courtesy of the Peoples Republic of China. *Page 24,* Photo by Emil Schulthes. *Page 26,* Pottery Factory, Foshan near Canton. Photo by Terry Madison/Image Bank. *Exhibit Photos* pages 29-75 courtesy of the Peoples Republic of China.

Select Bibliography

1. Hildburgh, W.L. "Chinese Utilizations of Parti-coloured Hard Stones. *Burlington Magazine,* 1942.

2. Hu, Chang-tu. *China: Its People, Its Society, Its Culture.* New Haven, HRAF Press, 1960.

3. Latourette, Kenneth Scott. *The Chinese: Their History & Culture.* New York, Macmillan Co., 1964.

4. Lin Yutang, *The Chinese Theory of Art,* Peking, Foreign Languages Press, 1967.

5. Liu, Wu-chi. *An Introduction to Chinese Literature.* Bloomington & London, Indiana University Press, 1966.

6. Medley, Margaret. *A Handbook of Chinese Art.* London, G. Bell & Sons, Ltd., 1964.

7. Pang Hsun-chin, Professor, Central Academy of Fine Arts. *Peoples China,* Peking, Foreign Languages Press, 1954.

8. Skoggard, Ross. "Report from China: Chinese Art, from Tao to Mao". *Art in America* 64: 1976.

9. Sullivan, Michael. *Chinese Art: Recent Discoveries.* London, Thames & Hudson, 1973.

10. Yang, Winston, L.Y.; Li, Peter; and Mao, Nathan K. *Classical Chinese Fiction.* Boston, G.K. Hall & Co., 1978.

11. Zung, Cecilia Sieu Ling. *Secrets of the Chinese Drama.* reissued: New York, Benjamin Blom, Inc., 1964.

12. *Chinese Arts & Crafts.* Peking, Light Industry Publ. House, Foreign Language Press, 1973.

Credits

Editor —————————————————————— John Dryden
Associate Editor —————————————————— Catherine Judd
Art Direction ————————————————— Consuelo Yznaga Regan
Book Designed by ——————————————— Carl T. Herrman
Cultural Consultant ——————————————————— Tsung Chin
Research and Production Assistance ——————— Elizabeth E. Warner
Chinese Translator ———————————————————— Robert Dunn
Editorial Advisor ——————————————————————— Paul Leung

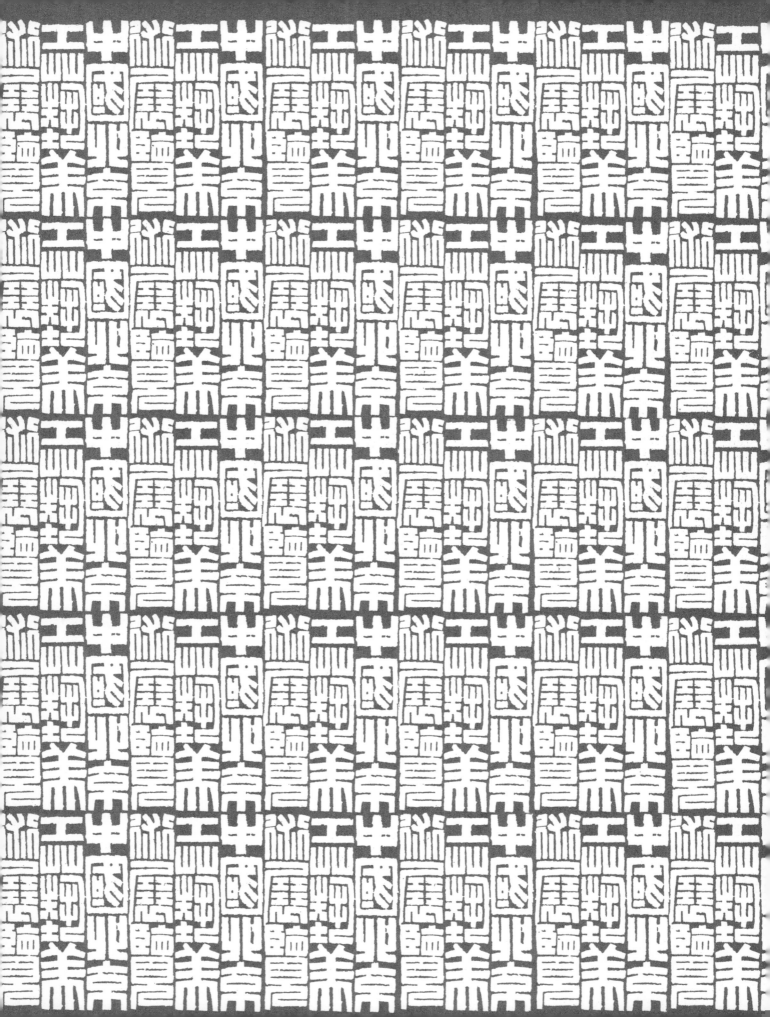